t f k	b c d	t y l
p g j	z s n	d b k
c n h	m n w	p qu g

Name _____

Initial Consonants   Circle the letter that stands for the first sound in each picture name.

1

f x t p b s g n l

Final Consonants   Write the letter that stands for the last sound in each picture name.

g		r
p		l
v		d

g		s
p		x
j		p

f		d
l	**5**	v
h		b

l		t
n		s
h		f

p		v
s	**6**	x
y		b

h		n
c		m
b		f

Name _____

Initial and Final Consonants Circle the letters that stand for the first sound and the last sound in each picture name.

3

l g f b t d	k d h n b m
k r g t j v	qu s g t p g
d k b t h l	h r qu b k n

4   **Initial and Final Consonants**   Circle the letters that stand for the first sound and the last sound in each picture name.

A a

apple

Name _____

Initial Short a Trace and write the letters. Color the pictures whose names begin with the short *a* sound.

5

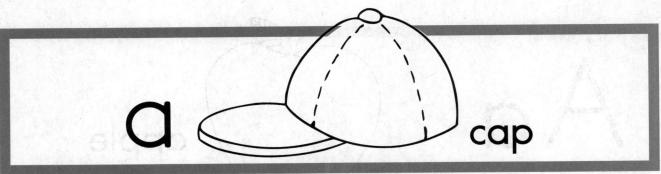

a   cap

6   **Medial Short a**   Color the pictures whose names have the short *a* sound.

Name _____

Initial and Medial Short a   Write *a* below each picture whose name has the short *a* sound.

7

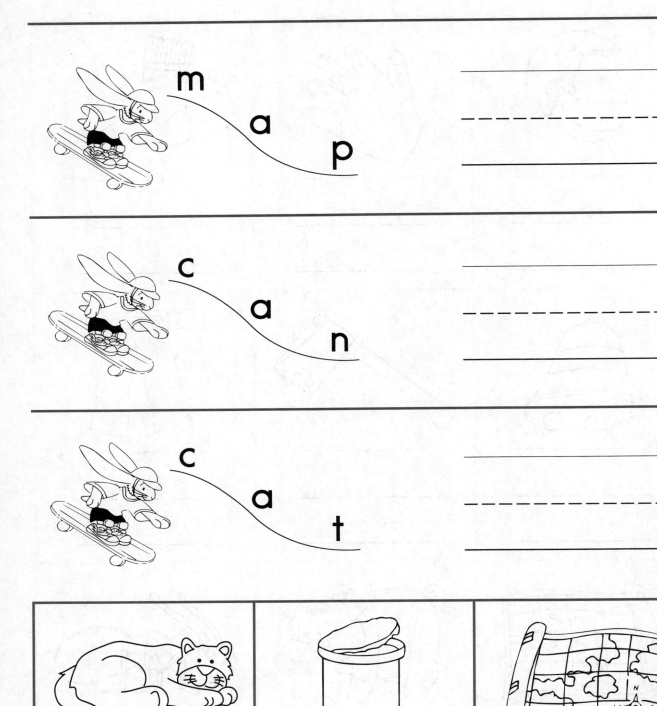

m a p

c a n

c a t

8   **Blending Short a Words**   Blend each word, and write it on the line. Then write the word that names each picture.

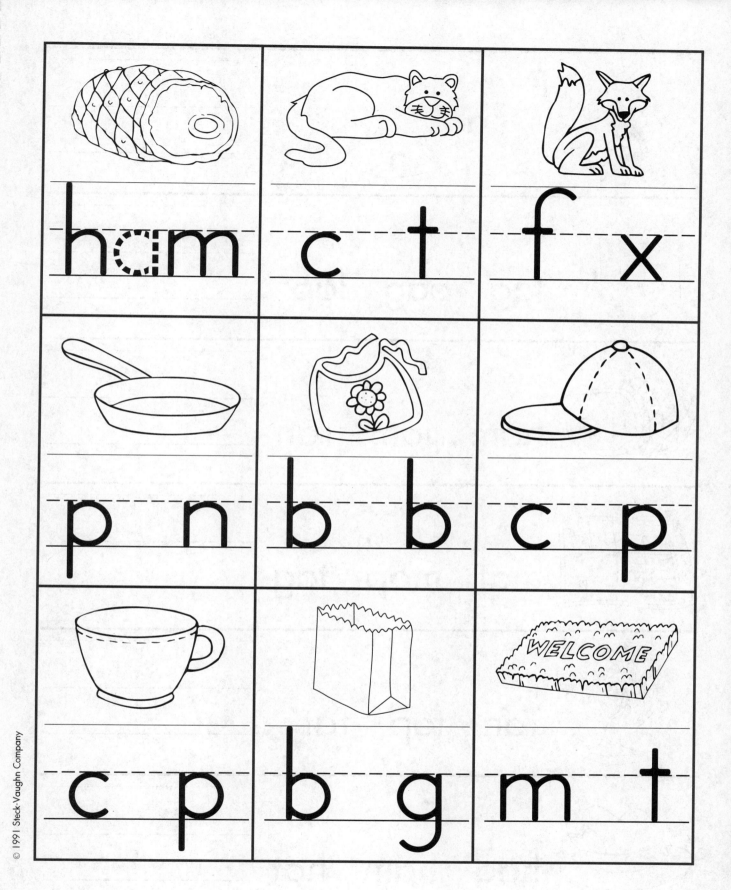

h a m	c _ t	f _ x
p _ n	b _ b	c _ p
c _ p	b _ g	m _ t

Name _____

Completing Short a Words Write *a* to complete each word whose name has the short *a* sound.

9

p

a

n

tag   bag   lap

ham   jam   ran

mat   map   tag

fan   tap   fat

had   ham   hat

© 1991 Steck-Vaughn Company

10   **Recognizing Short a Words** Blend and write the first word. Then circle the word that names each picture, and write it on the line.

| cat | pan | tag | cap |
| hat | bag | man | ham |

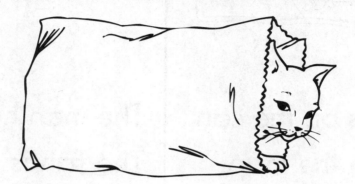

The cat is in the bag.

The ham is in the pan.

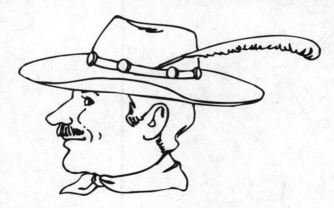

The tag is on the cap.

The hat is on the man.

Name _____

Short a Words and Sentences Review the words and their pictures. Underline the sentence that tells about each large picture.

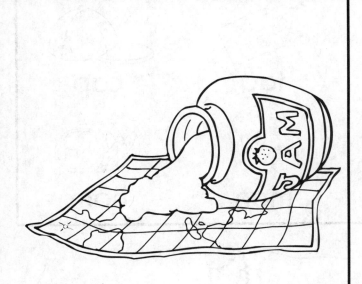

The tag is on the can.
Jam is on the map.

The man has a bat.
The fan is on the mat.

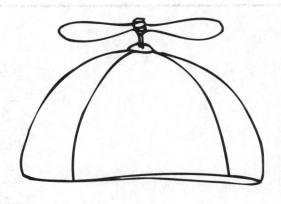

The cat sat on the hat.
Pat is mad at the cat.

The fan is on the cap.
Dan has the bag.

Short a Sentences Underline the sentence that tells about each picture.

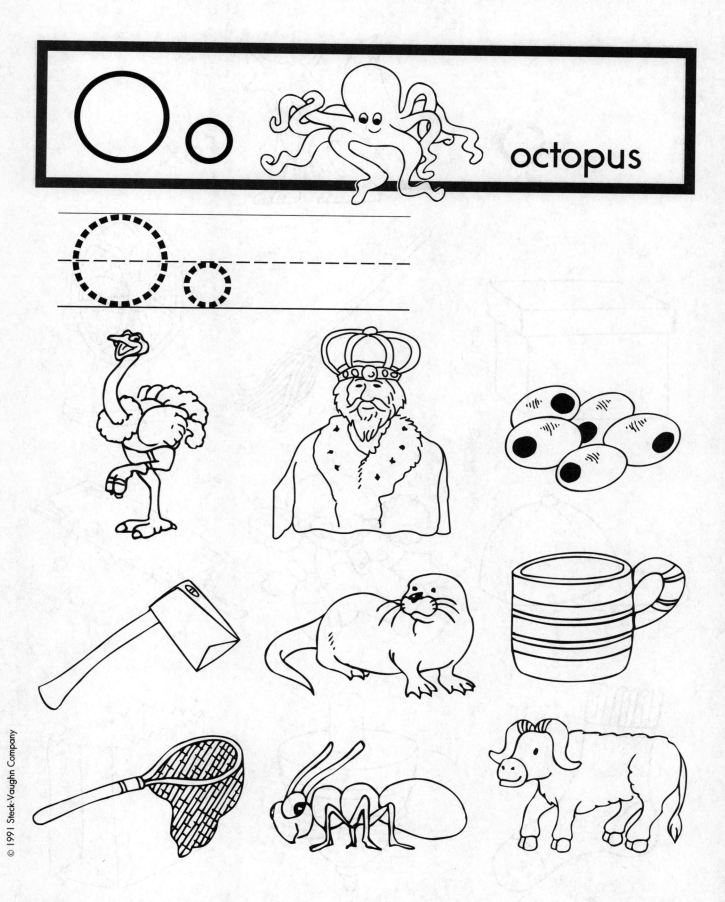

octopus

Name _____

Initial Short o Trace and write the letters. Color the pictures whose names begin with the short *o* sound.

13

O   fox

Medial Short o   Color the pictures whose names have the short o sound.

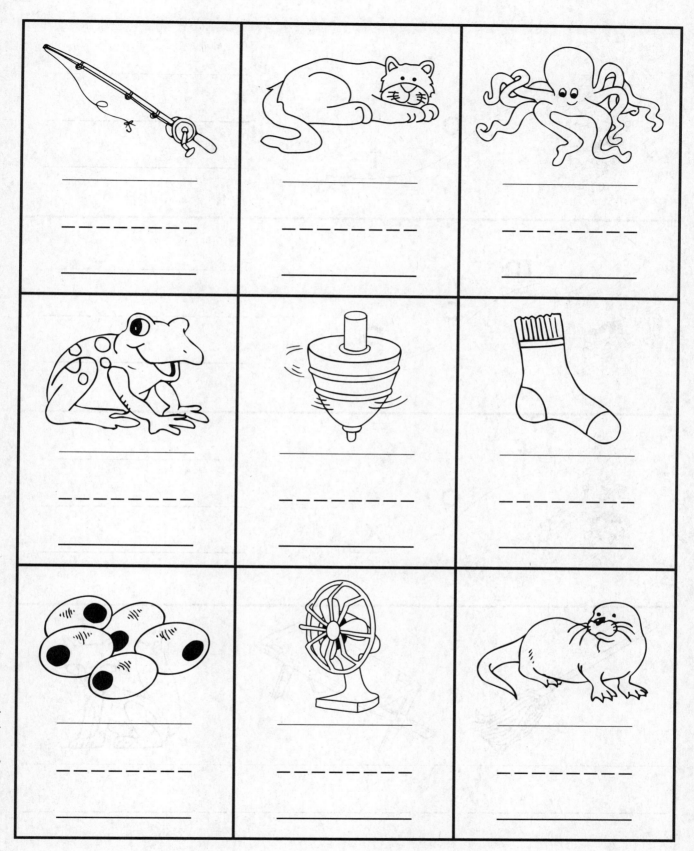

Name

Initial and Medial Short o   Write *o* below each picture whose name has the short *o* sound.

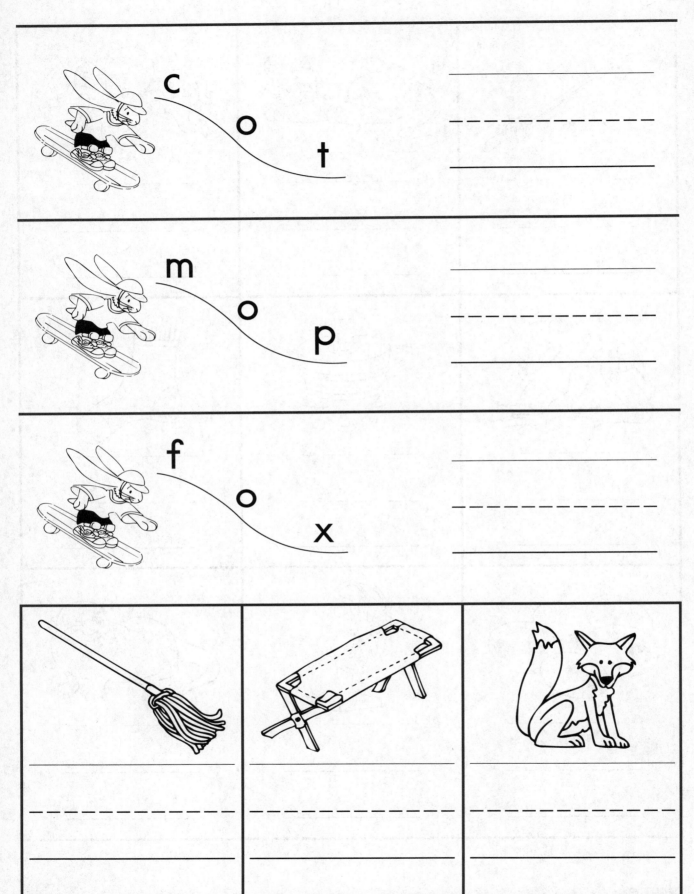

c   o   t

m   o   p

f   o   x

© 1991 Steck-Vaughn Company

Blending Short o Words Blend each word, and write it on the line. Then write the word that names each picture.

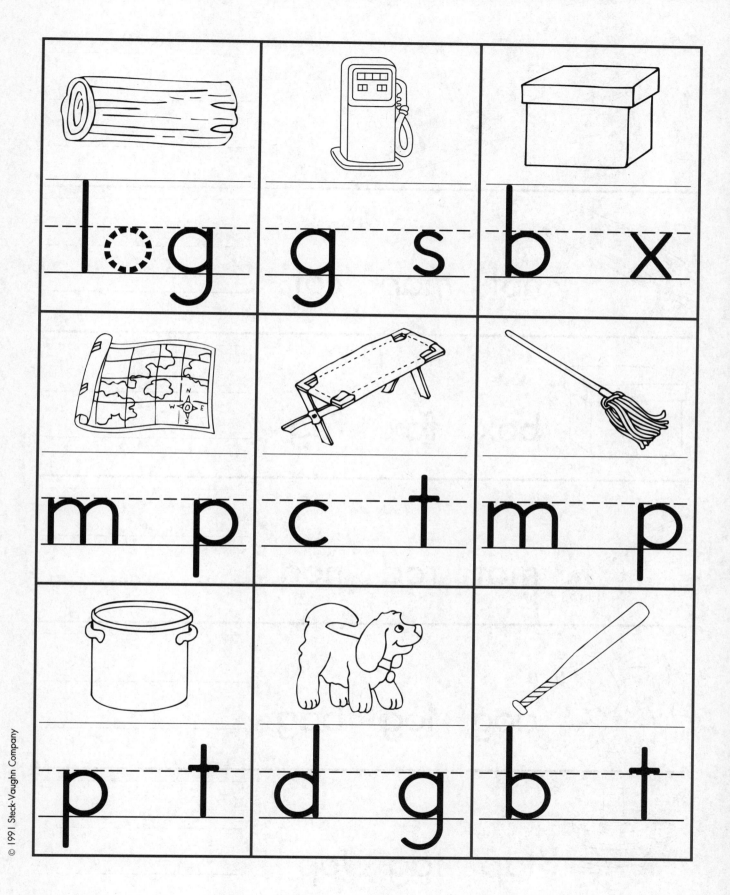

l o g g s b x

m p c t m p

p t d g b t

Name

Completing Short o Words Write *o* to complete each word whose name has the short *o* sound.

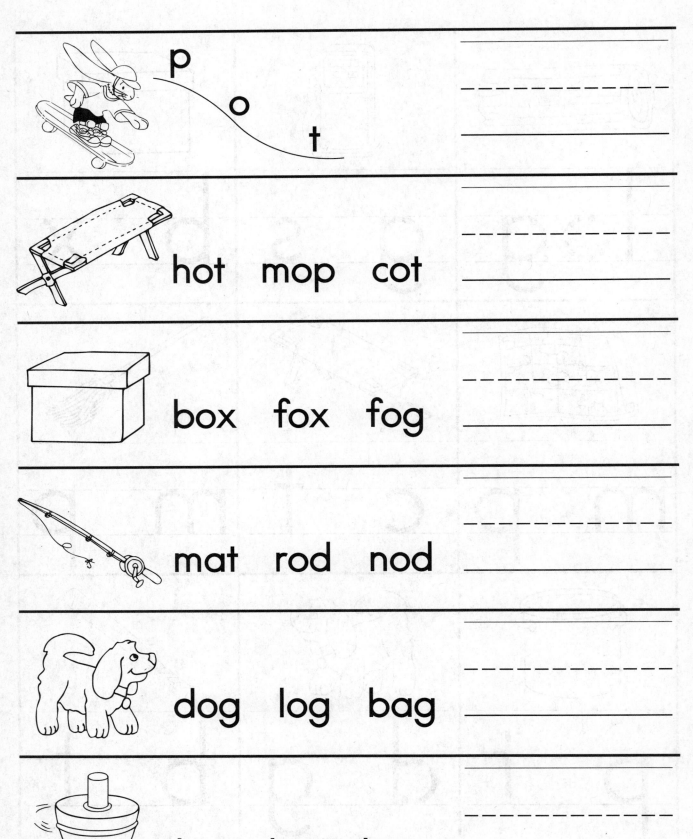

p o t

hot mop cot

box fox fog

mat rod nod

dog log bag

tap tag top

18 **Recognizing Short o Words** Blend and write the first word. Then circle the word that names each picture, and write it on the line.

rod	dog	top	fox
log	box	cot	pot

A fox is on the log.

A top is on the pot.

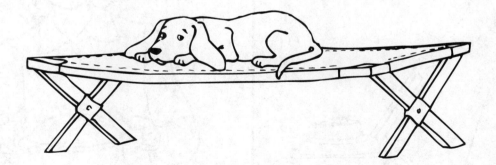

The rod is on the box.

The dog is on the cot.

Name _____

© 1991 Steck-Vaughn Company

Short o Words and Sentences Review the words and their pictures. Underline the sentence that tells about each large picture.

The man got a cot.

Bob can mop.

Don can hop and jog.

The dog got on a log.

The dog is in a box.

Tom got a job.

Mom got a hot pot.

Rob got the top.

20 **Short o Sentences** Underline the sentence that tells about each picture.

© 1991 Steck-Vaughn Company

I i   igloo

Name _____

Initial Short i Trace and write the letters. Color the pictures whose names begin with the short *i* sound.

21

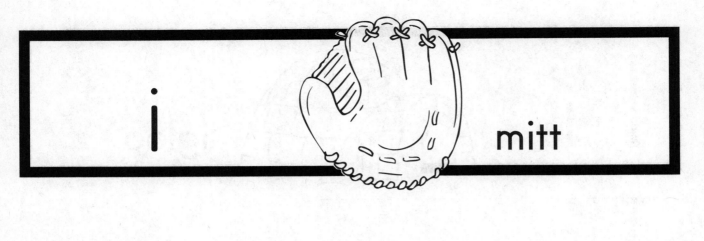

i   mitt

Medial Short i   Color the pictures whose names have the short *i* sound.

Initial and Medial Short i   Write *i* below each picture whose name has the short *i* sound.

p i g

l i d

b i b

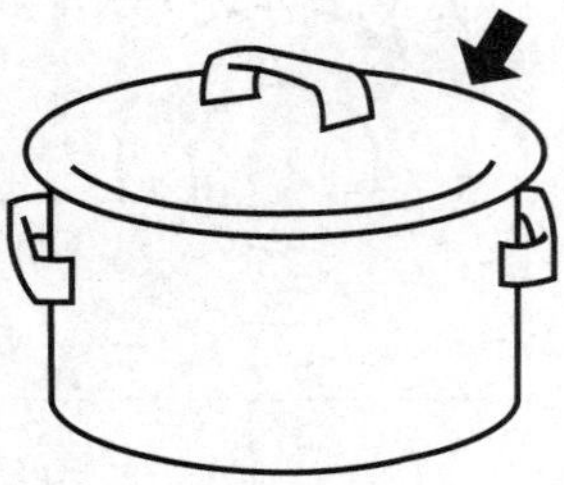

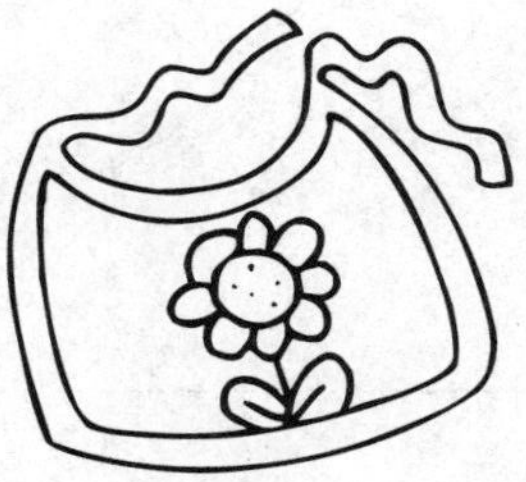

Blending Short i Words Blend each word, and write it on the line. Then write the word that names each picture.

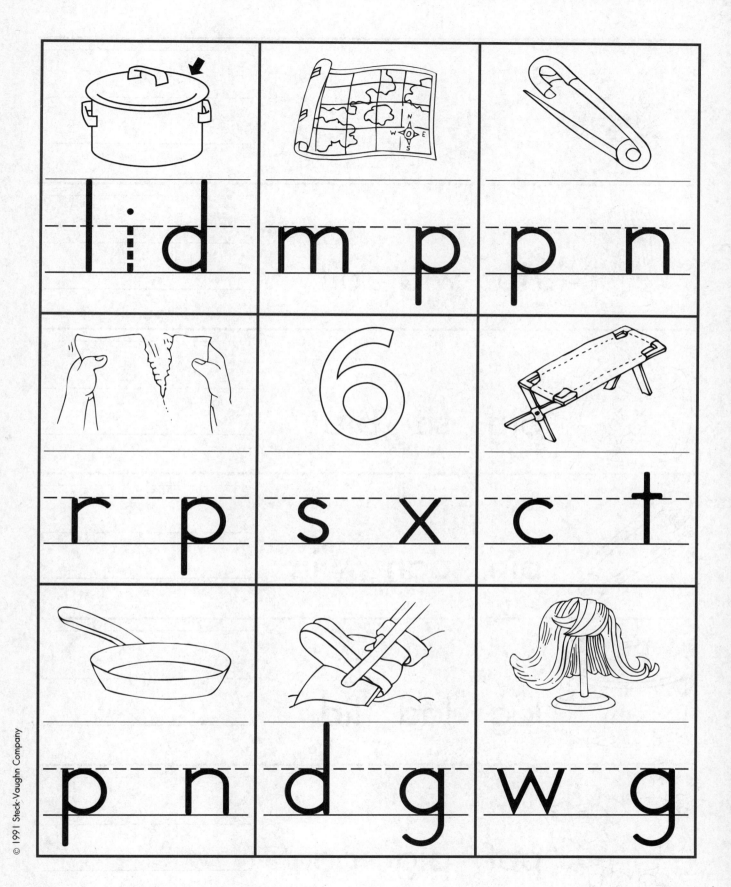

l i d	m p	p n
r p	s x	c t
p n	d g	w g

Name _____

Completing Short i Words Write *i* to complete each word whose name has the short *i* sound.

25

s i x

rib   wig   pit

big   sit   bib

pin   pan   win

log   lad   lid

pot   pig   pan

26   **Recognizing Short i Words**   Blend and write the first word. Then circle the word that names each picture, and write it on the line.

Jim	Kim	bib	rip
dig	pig	mitt	wig

Kim has a mitt.

Jim has a wig.

The bib can rip.

The pig can dig.

Name _____

Short i Words and Sentences Review the words and their pictures. Underline the sentence that tells about each large picture.

Kim can win.

Jim got a sip.

Tim has on a bib.

Sid got a mitt.

The wig is big.

The bib has a rip.

The dog got a rib.

A pig hid in a pit.

Short i Sentences Underline the sentence that tells about each picture.

Uu

umbrella

U u

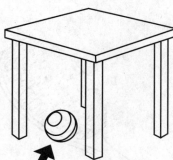

Name _____

Initial Short u Trace and write the letters. Color the pictures whose names begin with the short *u* sound.

29

u  cup

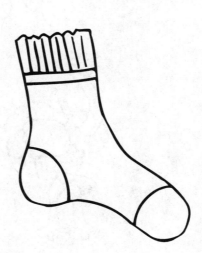

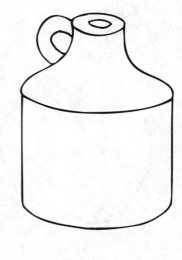

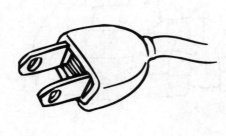

© 1991 Steck-Vaughn Company

30 **Medial Short u** Color the pictures whose names have the short *u* sound.

Name _____

Initial and Medial Short u   Write *u* below each picture whose name has the short *u* sound.

31

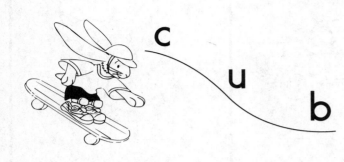

c u b

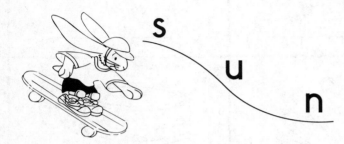

s u n

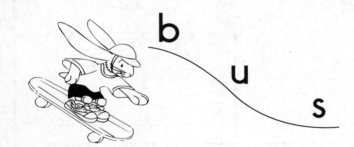

b u s

Blending Short u Words Blend each word, and write it on the line. Then write the word that names each picture.

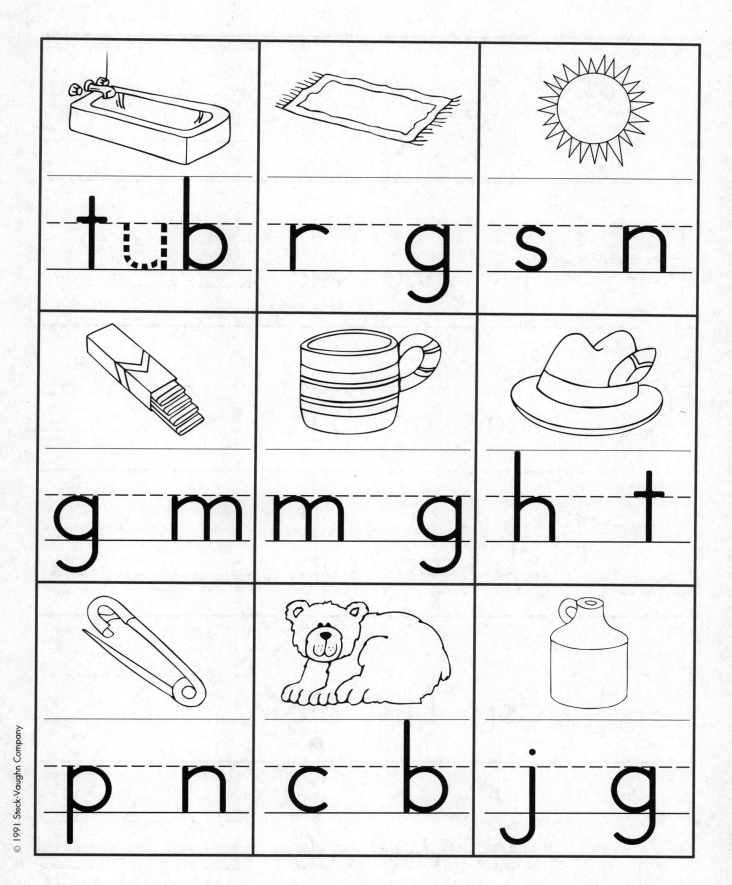

t u b   r   g   s   n

g   m   m   g   h   t

p   n   c   b   j   g

Name _____

Completing Short u Words Write *u* to complete each word whose name has the short *u* sound.

33

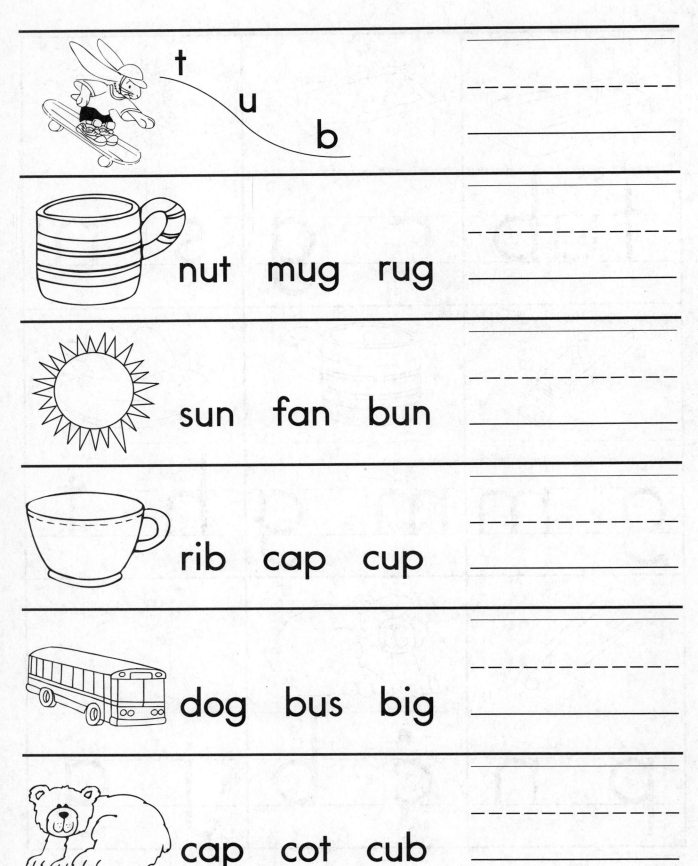

t
u
b

nut mug rug

sun fan bun

rib cap cup

dog bus big

cap cot cub

Recognizing Short u Words Blend and write the first word. Then circle the word that names each picture, and write it on the line.

cup   sun   cub   rug

bus   pup   gum   tub

The cub is in the tub.

The bus is in the sun.

The gum is on a cup.

The pup is on a rug.

© 1991 Steck-Vaughn Company

Name _____

Short u Words and Sentences   Review the words and their pictures. Underline the sentence that tells about each large picture.

35

The bus is in the sun.

The bug is on a jug.

Pam will hug the cub.

Bud will rub the pup.

A jug is in the tub.

The pig has fun in mud.

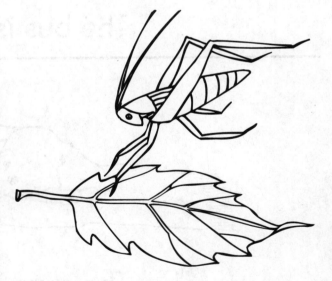

The pup will run.

The bug can hop.

Short u Sentences Underline the sentence that tells about each picture.

E e

egg

Name _____

Initial Short e Trace and write the letters. Color the pictures whose names begin with the short *e* sound.

37

e

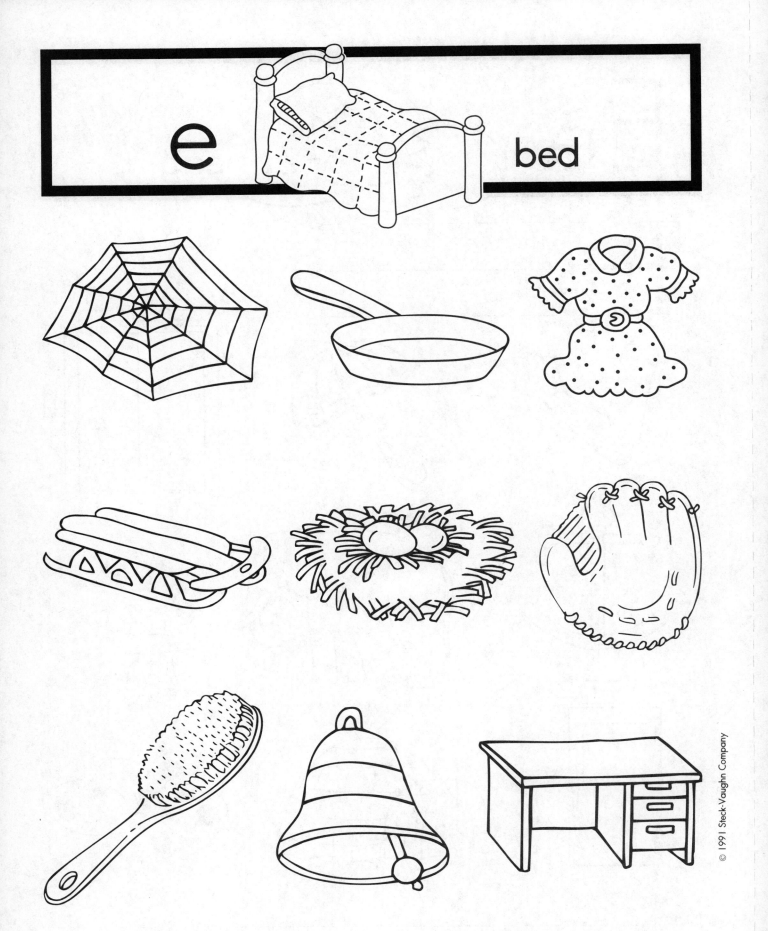

bed

Medial Short e Color the pictures whose names have the short *e* sound.

Name _____

Initial and Medial Short e   Write *e* below each picture whose name has the short *e* sound.

39

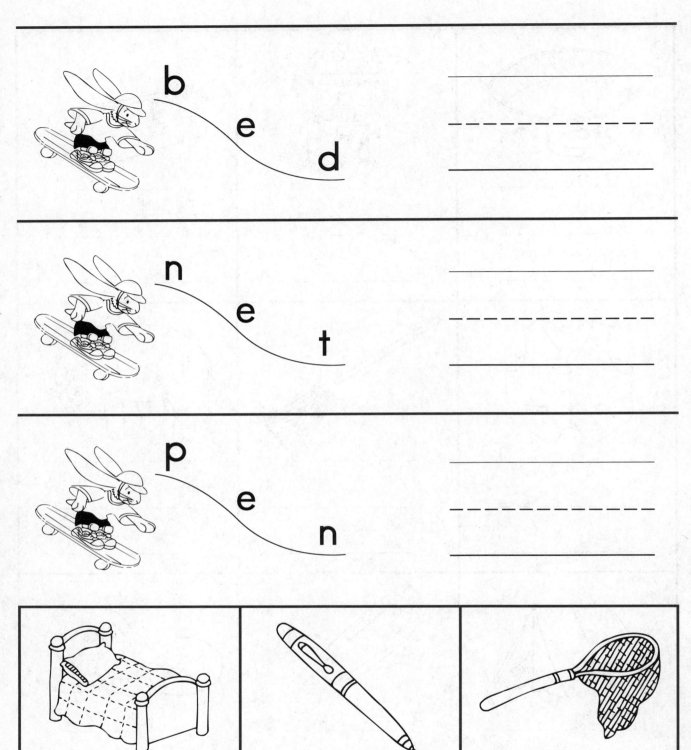

b e d

n e t

p e n

Blending Short e Words Blend each word, and write it on the line. Then write the word that names each picture.

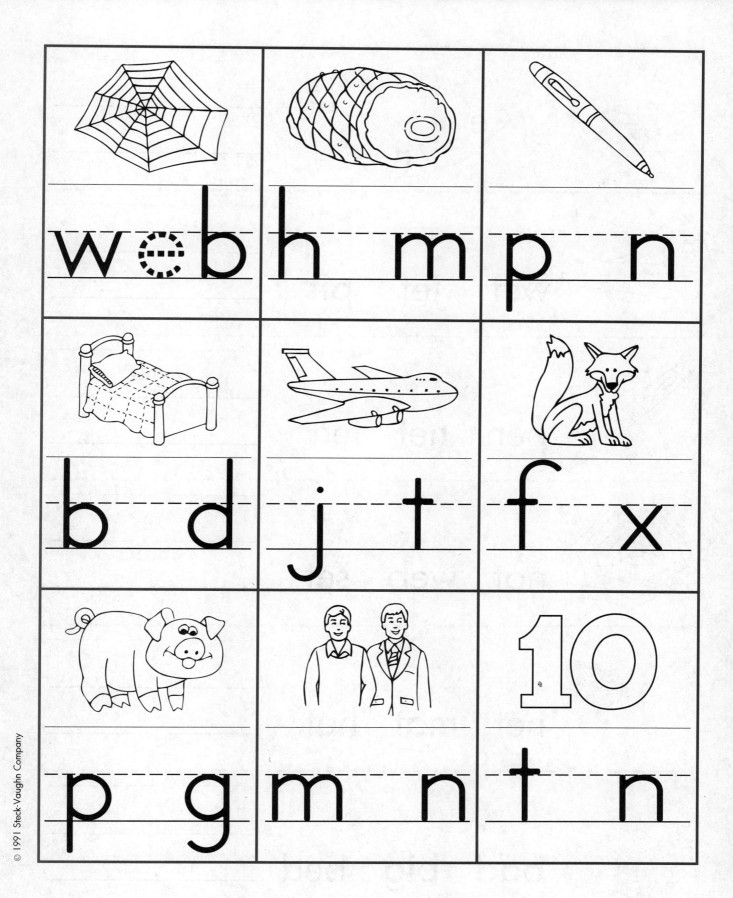

w e b	h m p	n
b d	j t	f x
p g	m n	t n

Name _____

Completing Short e Words Write *e* to complete each word whose name has the short *e* sound.

41

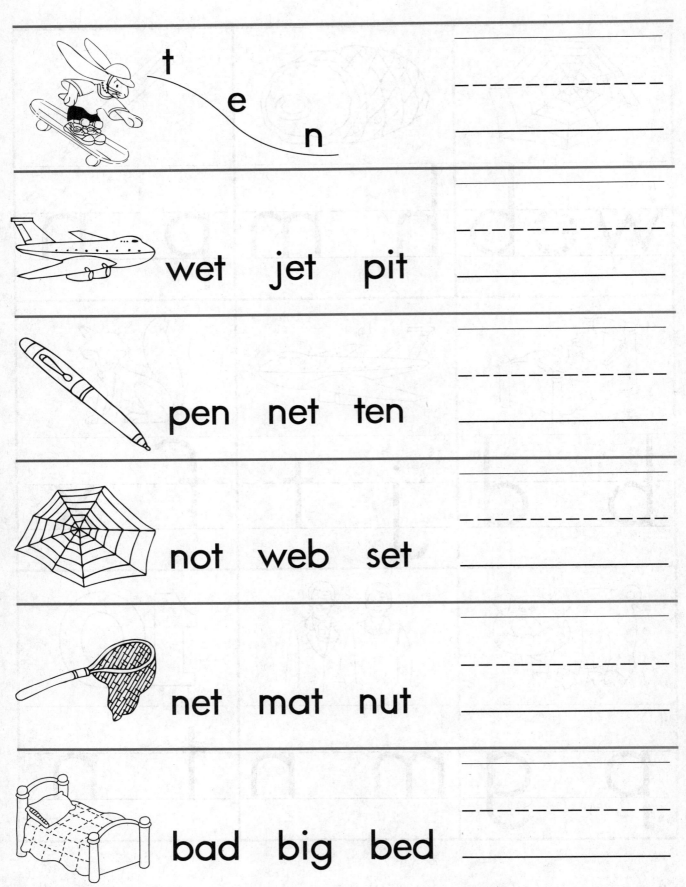

t

e

n

wet   jet   pit

pen   net   ten

not   web   set

net   mat   nut

bad   big   bed

Recognizing Short e Words   Blend and write the first word. Then circle the word that names each picture, and write it on the line.

Ben   leg   men   Meg

bed   hen   pen   wet   jet

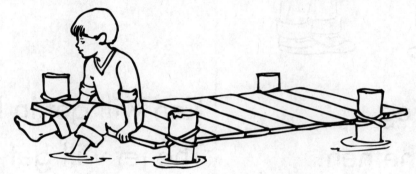

Ben has a wet leg.

Meg has a hen.

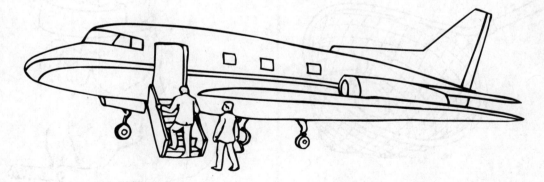

The pen is on the bed.

The men get on a jet.

Name _____

Short e Words and Sentences   Review the words and their pictures. Underline the sentence that tells about each large picture.

43

Ted met Peg.
Peg fed the hen.

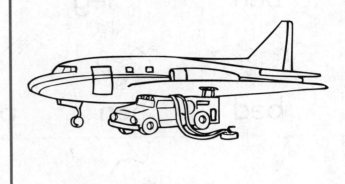

Ken will get in bed.
The jet will get gas.

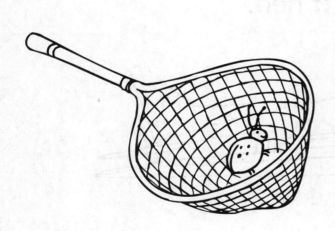

A red bug is in the net.
The hen is in a pen.

A pet will get fed.
Ted set a cot in the den.

Short e Sentences   Underline the sentence that tells about each picture.

cat cub can _____

peg pit pig _____

ham hat hut _____

tag tab tub _____

mop map men _____

bib bed bad _____

Name _____

Reviewing Short Vowel Words Circle the word that names each picture, and write it on the line.

bag   bug   bat   _____

fin   fan   fun   _____

wag   wet   wig   _____

net   nut   nap   _____

cap   cot   cup   _____

leg   log   lid   _____

Reviewing Short Vowel Words Circle the word that names each picture, and write it on the line.

A fox hid in a log.
Rex ran to the bed.

Meg got in the mud.
A pin is on his hat.

Tom can pet the dog.
The cat is mad at Kim.

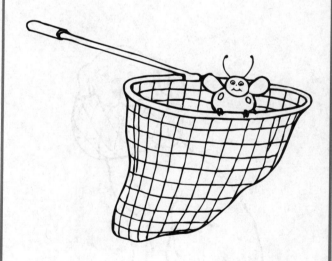

Jim has a map.
A fat bug is on a net.

Name _____

Reviewing Short Vowel Sentences   Underline the sentence that tells about each picture.

A wet pet is in the tub.
The red wig got wet.

Ted pins a tag on Pat.
Mom can fix the map.

Ben has a big ham.
The bun is not hot.

Meg is on the box.
Dad naps in the sun.

Reviewing Short Vowel Sentences Underline the sentence that tells about each picture.